HOW SMART ARE YOU?

TEST YOUR OWN IQ AGAIN

HOW SMART ARE YOU?

TEST YOUR OWN IQ AGAIN

NORMAN SULLIVAN

BLACK DOG & LEVENTHAL PUBLISHERS
NEW YORK

This edition, 1995, is published by arrangement with Sterling Publishing
Company, Inc., by

Black Dog & Leventhal Publishers Inc.
151 West 19th Street
New York, New York 10011

Distributed by

Workman Publishing Company
708 Broadway
New York, NY 10003

Manufactured in the United States of America

ISBN: 1-884822-18-5

h g f e d c b

CONTENTS

INTRODUCTION: Read this first, before you begin the tests

How smart are you? Have you ever taken an IQ test? What is intelligence, anyway? What has it to do with intuition, imagination, creativity—or any of the other special talents we honor? How can we quantify such a concept?

Any measure of intelligence inevitably involves a complex set of assumptions about what intelligence is and how it is valued in our society. Surveys have shown that most people rate intelligence among the highest values, along with health and wealth. Although tests of Intelligence Quotient, or IQ, have outgrown their original purpose (to predict academic success), they have survived and maintained a high status because they measure a quality deemed of great importance in society.

For more than a century, IQ tests have evoked controversy and met with conflict at every turn. The significance of the test and the fact that it provides a "scale" for intelligence has aroused highly charged emotions. Theories have been propounded that intelligence is influenced by environment, especially in the formative years, and by other factors. But heredity and environment never work in isolation; they always work in interaction with each other. So the primary argument comes down to determining what their ratio is in determining IQ score.

IQ tests have been implemented in American education, and have been used in colleges, graduate programs, businesses, and corporations. At the outset it may seem useful and fortunate that we have a standardized measure with which to gauge people. Unfortunately, however, no one has been able to substantiate fully the correlation between IQ tests and intelligence.

Even if we separate IQ tests from the issue of intelligence, can we condone using the scores as a basis for selecting an individual for a particular position? This façade of practical usefulness may shroud a much deeper, fundamental problem in our society. Users of IQ tests must ask exactly what they are measuring, and whether the tests measure the same thing for all subjects. The most frequent and vehement attack against IQ tests charges that they are culturally biased against racial and ethnic minorities and the poor. No one test can be completely "objective" no matter how hard the test-maker tries.

We have attempted to make our book as "culturally neutral" as possible. This just means minimizing "culture loading" by avoiding the use of words or pictures that are more accessible to one group than another. Neutral elements used may include lines, curves, squares, and circles—involving universal concepts such as up/down, open/closed, right/left, whole/half, full/empty, larger/smaller, many/few, etc. More complex problems involve relational reasoning or figure-series completions and figural analogies.

Questions involving reasoning and deduction require the examination of a given premise and the inference of conclusions from that premise. Verbal skills tested involve knowing the meaning of words and how to spell them. Of course, this section requires some education and experience, so it is much more culturally loaded than some other areas. We have included the verbal section to make the tests more fun and challenging, while still attempting to eliminate highly biased entries.

FORMAT

This book features three sections—Elementary, Challenging, and Masterful, with sixty questions in each of the first two sections and forty-five in the third. The tests are meant to amuse and challenge you, certainly taxing your cerebral capacity.

The example below shows one type of question you'll find. It is not representative of all question types, but it does offer a clue to how the test requires you to think, and what kinds of things you should look for.

A popular type of question asks you to choose the "odd one out" from a group of words, shapes, symbols, etc. The test-maker must take care to ensure that the "odd one out" has an outstanding difference from the others, and that the distractors (the choices that are not "odd") are similar enough to the correct one to provide some challenge. Here is an example of the type of question that should *not* be given, because it would give rise to disagreement:

Which is the odd one out?

3 4 5 6 7 8

At first glance, there is no apparent answer. It is no use choosing any one number on the grounds that it is odd, even, or a prime number, since there are three of each. They all follow a straightforward arithmetic progression, so there is no clue there. What, then, is left? Let's spell out the numbers:

three four five six seven eight

Any clue here? Four—because the number of letters corresponds with the number itself; five—because it contains V, the Roman numeral for the number itself; eight—because it is the only word that starts with a vowel. You could think of other possible answers, but they are all weak, simply because no one number has any distinctive feature.

Here is a better example:

Which is the odd one out?

6 7 10 15 20 21

Your reasoning could follow these lines: is there a common divisor in all but one number? No. Is there a single odd or even number? No. What about a common sequence? No—they increase by 1, 3, 5, 5, 1. Nothing outstanding there. What, then, is the only number in the series that has a characteristic not shared by the others? The only such number is 7, because it is the only prime number. This is the sort of reasoning you will have to practice as you go through the tests. We are not trying to trick you; we are trying to challenge you.

You should begin by gathering writing materials—not only because some of the problems may require working-out on paper, but also because you should keep note of your answers and scores (these appear at the end of each individual test) until you have completed all the tests. At the end of the book is a

scoring chart with instructions on how to figure out your actual IQ, gauging your scores in relation to the majority of people in your age group.

Have a watch or clock handy so that you can time yourself during each test. Speed of answering is related to speed of comprehension, so each test has a time limit. A correct answer arrived at with little delay shows quicker comprehension, yet it is better to linger awhile and arrive at the correct answer, than to give the wrong answer quickly.

When the time limit is up you should stop recording your answers, even if you have not completed the test. (For your own interest, you might want to finish it, though.) The charm of this book is that you can choose to take tests adhering to the time limits, or you can go through the tests without regard to the time, simply viewing them as entertainment and pleasure—just as you would tackle a crossword puzzle to pass the time, in no particular hurry.

We hope we have offered brain-teasers you will find exciting and enlightening, while also providing you with an IQ scale you can use to evaluate yourself. Remembering that the IQ number game gauges what you have already learned, and not your capacity to learn, you can take advantage of it for sheerly enjoyable and entertaining purposes.

GROUP I

ELEMENTARY LEVEL

1 What letter will complete this word?

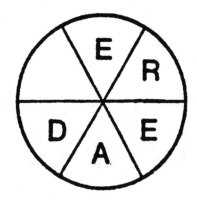

2 Which one of these figures is wrong?

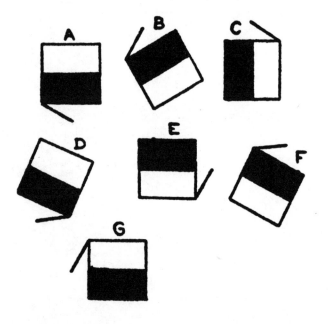

3 Add the two highest numbers and take away the sum of the three lowest numbers.

16	13	9	11	23	19
5	14	12	15	18	17

4 If 6 3 5 4 2 equals 5 2 6 3 4, what is:
B C D E F ?

5 Join these syllables in pairs to make ten words:

REC	LET	LOON	SORE
AD	BAL	TOM	FUR
ER	ORD	BRE	TAB
OR	CAT	EYE	HER
BOY	SA	OUT	LE

6 Arrange these into four pairs:

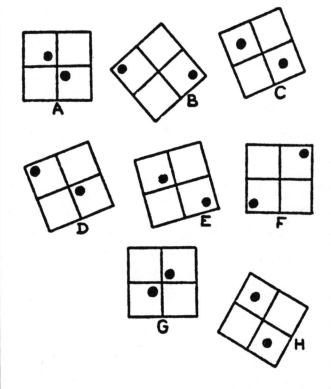

10

7 What are the last two terms in these series?

Z 13 Y 14 W 16 T 19 - -

---

8 Which is the odd one out?

(A) LIRA   (B) MARKS
(C) DRACHMAE   (D) RAND
(E) FRANCS

---

9 Which is the odd one out?

(A) Y L A P   (B) A P R E O
(C) V E E R U   (D) R E N C O C T
(E) S H E C S

---

10 Which of these is wrong?

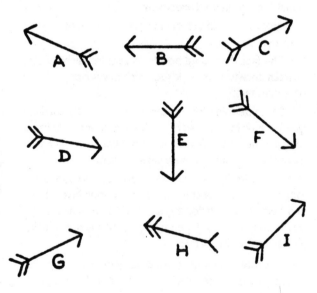

---

11 Which date does not conform with the others?

(A) 1584   (B) 1692
(C) 1729   (D) 1809
(E) 1980

---

12 Which is the odd one out?

(A) ELIGIBLE   (B) SHEEPISH
(C) DELIGHTED   (D) FOOLPROOF
(E) GNASHING

---

13 Arrange these words in alphabetical order:

(A) ABRACADABRA   (B) ABOUT
(C) ABBEY   (D) ABUNDANCE
(E) ABACUS   (F) ABOULIA
(G) ABBOT

---

14 Who has changed his expression?

---

15 Which of these shields are identical?

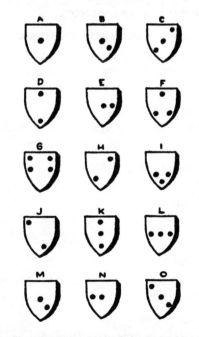

NOW CHECK YOUR ANSWERS AND KEEP A RECORD OF YOUR SCORE.

1 H (SCORE I POINT).

The word is ADHERE.

2 A (SCORE I POINT).

When the diagonal line from the base-line of the square inclines to the right, as in C, E, and G, the right half of the square is black.

When it inclines to the left, as in B, D, and F, the bottom half of the square is black.

In A, the right half of the square should be black.

3 17 (SCORE I POINT).

4 D F B C E (SCORE I POINT).

The letters must be transposed in the same order as the numbers.

5 (SCORE I POINT IF ALL ARE CORRECT; ½ POINT IF 8 ARE CORRECT).

REC-ORD	EYE-SORE
CAT-ER	OUT-LET
TOM-BOY	SA-LOON
TAB-LE	BRE-AD
HER-BAL	FUR-OR

6 AG   BF   CH   DE

(SCORE I POINT IF ALL ARE CORRECT).

7 P 23 (SCORE I POINT IF BOTH ARE CORRECT).

Two separate series. Letters descend alphabetically, first to the next letter, then skipping one, then two, and so on. The numbers rise in the same way.

8 (B) (SCORE I POINT).

All the other currencies contain the letters RA in that order. In MARKS these letters are reversed.

9 (E) (SCORE I POINT).

An anagram of CHESS. All the others are anagrams of types of entertainment:

(A) PLAY   (C) REVUE
(B) OPERA   (D) CONCERT

10 H (SCORE I POINT).

The point has two barbs instead of one, and one set of tail feathers instead of two.

11 (C) (SCORE I POINT).

The digits add up to 19. In all the others they add up to 18.

12 (B) (SCORE I POINT).

It starts and ends with the same two letters. All the others start and end with the same two letters reversed.

13 (E) (C) (G) (F) (B) (A) (D) (SCORE I POINT).

14 J (SCORE I POINT).

The mouth should be the same as in B and H.

15 B and M (SCORE I POINT).

Remember to record your score.

NOTES

Although all of the tests in this book are graded according to difficulty, in any one section some problems are more difficult (or easier) than others. The dividing line is slim between a difficult problem in one section and an easy one in the next. In the end, however, the final count of "easy" and "difficult" problems is immaterial, because the ultimate ratings are based on all the problems collectively.

In imposing time limits, two factors have been considered:

(1) The fact that some problems require fairly lengthy written answers (as opposed to simply writing a letter or a number);

(2) Some people write faster than others. Accordingly, where written answers are involved, not only has a longer time been allowed, but time has been taken from that of comparatively slow writers.

Number 5 in the previous test took our volunteers longer—because of the amount of writing involved, and because it calls for a great deal of "trial and error" deduction. Success depends largely on making a lucky guess among alternatives.

Other problems which caused delay in answering—or failure to answer correctly—were 8 and 12, each calling for deductions beyond the obvious. In the case of 8, the fact that one currency is non-European would not have been as strong an answer as the one given in the answer section.

1 What goes into the empty brackets?

144	(3625)	125
96	(1618)	126
112	( )	144

2 Fill in the brackets. The word in each set of brackets must logically follow the previous word and precede the following word, e.g., library (BOOK) mark.

BULL
( )
HOUSE
( )
YARD
( )
BATH
( )
FALL
( )
SIDE
( )
WAY

3 Using your eye only, which is the missing brick?

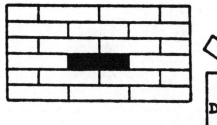
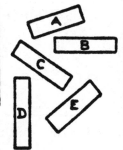

4 Which is the odd one out?

5 Arrange these strange-looking insects into four pairs:

6 What is X?

J - M - M - J - S - N - X

---

7 Which one is wrong?

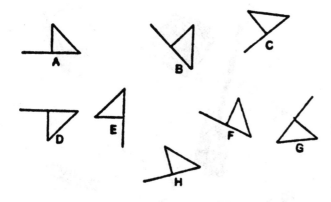

---

8 Arrange the labels into four pairs:

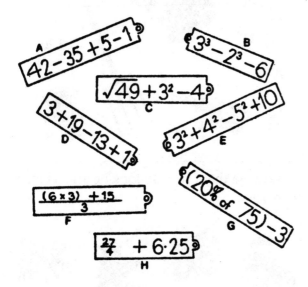

---

9 What is X?

---

10 Complete these words, for which definitions are given:

p	e	r							Staff
	p	e	r						Surgical treatment
		p	e	r					Take the place of
			p	e	r				Not much hope!
				p	e	r			Thrived
					p	e	r		They take off clothes or paint!
						p	e	r	Periodical

---

11 Arrange these patterns into four pairs.

---

12 Which of these does not belong?

4   18   16   8   24

13 Change RAIN into SNOW in three moves, changing TWO letters at a time.

```
  R A I N
1 _ _ _ _
2 _ _ _ _
3 S N O W
```

14 Which is the odd one out?

(A) PROVERBS
(B) RUTH
(C) EZEKIEL
(D) CORINTHIANS
(E) NUMBERS
(F) PSALMS

15 Assuming that the top two stars are correct, which of those below are wrong?

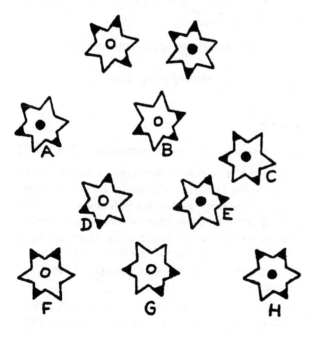

1 1416 (SCORE 1 POINT).

In the first example, divide the left-hand number by 4 and the right-hand number by 5.

In the second example, divide the left-hand number by 6 and the right-hand number by 7.

Therefore, in the third line, divide the left-hand number by 8(14) and the right-hand number by 9(16).

2 DOG - BOAT - BIRD - WATER - OUT - WALK (SCORE 1 POINT IF ALL ARE CORRECT).

3 C (SCORE 1 POINT).

4 F (SCORE 1 POINT).

The others pair as follows: A and L; B and K; C and J; D and H; E and I; G and M. The comb does not pair with anything.

5 AF BG CH DE (SCORE 1 POINT).

6 J (SCORE 1 POINT).

The initials are the months of the year. The sequence is every two months: January, March, May, etc. The answer is J for January.

7 D (SCORE 1 POINT).

The triangle should be on the right-hand side of the base-line.

8 AF BH CG DE (SCORE 1 POINT).

A and F each equal 11.
B and H each equal 13.
C and G each equal 12.
D and E each equal 10.

9 B (SCORE 1 POINT).

In each section, the letters in the outer ring combine with those in the inner ring to form a word in conjunction with LAND, which is common to all the words:

IS	LAND	ER
G	LAND	ULAR
OUT	LAND	ISH
UP	LAND	S
S	LAND	ER
GAR	LAND	S
B	LAND	ISHMENT (X is B)

10 (SCORE 1 POINT IF ALL ARE CORRECT; SCORE ½ POINT IF 6 ARE CORRECT.)

PERSONNEL	PROSPERED
OPERATION	STRIPPERS
SUPERCEDE	NEWSPAPER
DESPERATE	

11 AE BD CG FH (SCORE 1 POINT).

12 18 (SCORE 1 POINT).

All the others are divisible by 4.

13 (SCORE 1 POINT FOR THE FOLLOWING, OR FOR OTHER WORDS, PROVIDED THEY ARE REAL WORDS AND FULFILL THE REQUIREMENT OF CHANGING **TWO** LETTERS AT A TIME):

	R A I N
1	S A I L
2	S N I P
3	S N O W

14 (D) (SCORE 1 POINT).

CORINTHIANS is in the New Testament; all the others are in the Old Testament.

15 F and H (SCORE 1 POINT IF BOTH CORRECT).

Remember to record your score.

NOTES

Most time was lost by the volunteers on 1, 2, 8, and 13.

Few were able to solve 1 within the time limit, yet one person arrived at the answer almost immediately. He was a mathematics teacher at a high school! The relationship between the numbers outside the brackets and those inside struck him instantly, substantiating the fact that one person will excel in a subject for which a special aptitude is an advantage, whereas another will be stumped by it.

Obviously, 8 took some time to solve, as each of the mathematical problems had to be solved individually.

In 13, the necessity for changing TWO letters at a time created considerable confusion.

1 What are x and y?

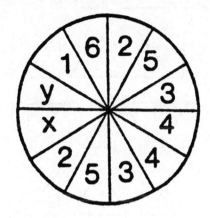

2 Which is the odd one out?

(A) CABBAGE
(B) HAPPY
(C) FELLOW
(D) KURSAAL
(E) GLIMMER

3 Complete words to fit the definitions. The number of missing letters is indicated by dashes.

HAPPEN	- - - - - - I R E
DRESS	- - - I R E
PLOT	- - - - - I R E
DIE	- - - I R E
WHOLE	- - - I R E
DOMINION	- - - I R E
BOG	- - - - - I R E
LAMPOON	- - - I R E
ARBITRATOR	- - - I R E

4 If is superimposed on

which of the OUTLINES below will result?

5 Which column does not conform?

A	B	C	D	E	F
17	14	22	31	29	33
9	13	15	22	19	8
13	11	17	17	31	19
24	7	2	13	5	20
2	29	8	4	2	17
10	6	21	3	10	3

6 If the figure below were held in front of a mirror and the mirror turned upside-down, which of the other figures would be reflected?

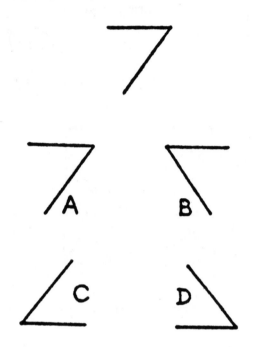

7 Which is the odd one out?

(A) STARLING
(B) PARTRIDGE
(C) GROUSE
(D) BLUETIT
(E) CUCKOO-PINT
(F) LARK
(G) NIGHTINGALE

8 Which row is wrong?

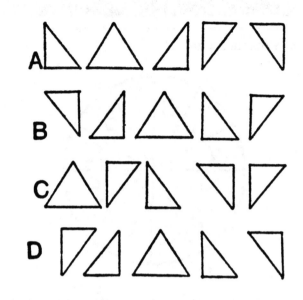

9 What is two days after the day after the day before yesterday?

10 Which is the odd word out?

(A) MEDICAL
(B) BATTLE
(C) ARTICLE
(D) BALLET
(E) RECITAL
(F) CLAIMED
(G) TABLET

11 Give words described by these definitions. Each word must contain AND.

(A) Evergreen shrub
(B) Lizard-like animal
(C) Stray
(D) Footwear
(E) Baton
(F) Part of Scotland
(G) Sweets
(H) Have many love affairs
(I) Spend wastefully
(J) Strainer

12 Which trellis is wrong?

13 If 3(76) equals 212 and 4(320) equals 125 what is 5(6100)?

14 Without turning the page upside down, which of these numbers will **not** read the same when turned upside-down?

A 81 691 8

B 81 81 8

C 1 89981

D 1 16911

E 196961

15 One of these words is spelled incorrectly. Which one?

(A) RECEIVE
(B) IMMANENT
(C) FASCIA
(D) DESSICATED
(E) BUDGERIGAR
(F) SCHISM
(G) PNEUMONIA
(H) NASCENT
(I) LEMUR
(J) CHEETAH

NOW CHECK YOUR ANSWERS AND KEEP A RECORD OF YOUR SCORE.

1 X is 6; Y is 1 (SCORE 1 POINT IF BOTH ARE CORRECT).
Starting at number 1 and moving to alternate segments clockwise:

1   2   3   4   5   6

Starting at number 6 and moving the same way:

6   5   4   3   2   1

2 (D) (SCORE 1 POINT).
In KURSAAL there are two identical adjacent vowels. In all the other words there are two identical adjacent consonants.

3 (SCORE 1 POINT IF ALL ARE CORRECT; ½ IF 7 OR 8 ARE CORRECT.)
TRANSPIRE
ATTIRE
CONSPIRE
EXPIRE
ENTIRE
EMPIRE
QUAGMIRE
SATIRE
UMPIRE

4 B (SCORE 1 POINT).

5 E (SCORE 1 POINT).
Adding up each column:

Column A	75	Column D	90
Column B	80	Column E	96
Column C	85	Column F	100

6 B (SCORE 1 POINT).
The fact that the MIRROR (not the figure!) is held upside-down will make no difference to the reflection.

7 (E) (SCORE 1 POINT).
CUCKOO-PINT is a flower—the more commonly known arum or wake-robin. All the others are birds.

8 C (SCORE 1 POINT).
Except for C, each row contains 1 equilateral triangle, 2 right-angled triangles with the base at the bottom and 2 with the base at the top.

In C there are 3 right-angled triangles with the base at the top and only one with the base at the bottom.

9 Tomorrow (SCORE 1 POINT).
The day before yesterday was two days ago; the day after yesterday was yesterday; two days after that (yesterday) is TOMORROW.

10 (D) (SCORE 1 POINT).
Apart from this, the words are paired in anagrams:
(A) MEDICAL with (F) CLAIMED
(B) BATTLE with (G) TABLET
(C) ARTICLE with (E) RECITAL
No word shown forms an anagram with BALLET.

11 (SCORE 1 POINT IF ALL ARE CORRECT; ½ POINT IF 8 OR 9 ARE CORRECT.)
(A) OLEANDER   (F) HIGHLANDS or LOWLANDS
(B) SALAMANDER (G) CANDY
(C) WANDER   (H) PHILANDER
(D) SANDAL   (I) SQUANDER
(E) WAND   (J) COLANDER

12 E (SCORE 1 POINT).
The diagonal slat from top left to bottom right should pass under the other slats.

13 3020 (SCORE 1 POINT).
The first two digits on the right side of the brackets are divided by the digit on the left to give the first digit inside the brackets.

The remaining number on the right of the brackets is multiplied by the digit on the left side of the brackets to give the remaining number inside the brackets.

14 C (SCORE 1 POINT).

15 (D) (SCORE 1 POINT).
This should be spelled: DESICCATED.

Remember to record your score.

NOTES

Questions 3 and 11 called for a fair amount of writing, which is allowed for in the time limit.

A few volunteers were stumped by 6, jumping at what appeared to be the obvious, but overlooking the vital fact that the reversal of the mirror makes no difference to the reflection.

Many lost points on 7 and 11; in the latter, (A), (B), (H), and (J) caused most trouble.

In 15, the fairly well-recognized general weakness in spelling was revealed. Remarkably, two *chefs* failed to spot that DESICCATED was spelled incorrectly!

1 Which of the symbols at the bottom should take the place of X?

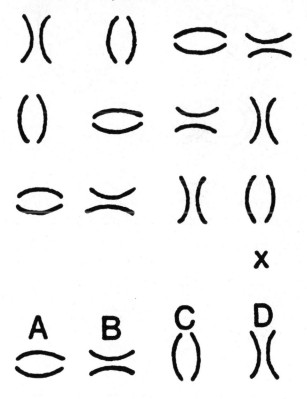

2 What is X?

2	1	8	5	9
3	7	2	6	2
4	2	1	1	X

3 Supply the missing letter. (Proper nouns not allowed!)

4 Which is the odd one out?

(A) SHORE   (C) TUTOR

(B) KEPI   (D) ASSB

5 Which letter does not conform with the others?

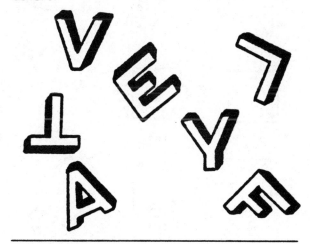

6 What WORD is represented by X?

31   31   X   31

7 Which is the odd one out?

(A) TESTAMENT   (D) GRAVAMEN

(B) PROMINENCE   (E) FLAMENCO

(C) FILAMENT   (F) STAMENS

8 Give words to fit these definitions. Each word must contain a part of the body:

(A) Apparatus for applying mechanical power

(B) Fast time for a musician

(C) Gardener's means of transport

(D) Uttering of speech

(E) Nautical pal

(F) Security device

21

9 Arrange these into six pairs:

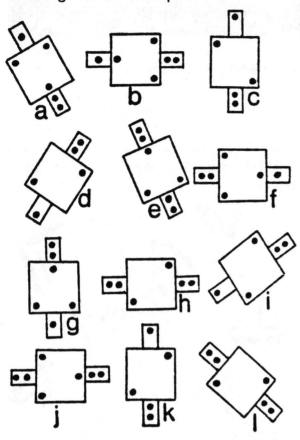

10 What is X?

3   6   10   15   X   28

11 Give words to fit these definitions. Each word must start with the last two letters of the previous word.

(A) STAR
(B) FISH
(C) END OF THE LINE
(D) CUSTOMARY PRACTICE
(E) ARMY OFFICER
(F) DIVORCE ALLOWANCE
(G) SYNTHETIC FIBER
(H) ATTACK
(I) WORD EXPERT
(J) THOROUGHFARE

12 Which are the weak links?

13 What four-letter word placed inside the brackets will complete all of these words?

A (- - - -) N T
S U B (- - - -)
(- - - -) R I C K

14 What are X and Y?

7   8   6   9   5   10   X   Y   3   12

15 Arrange these shapes in order according to the number of sides, starting with the one with the least number:

(A) OCTAGON
(B) HEXAGON
(C) PENTAGON
(D) DECAGON
(E) TETRAGON
(F) NONAGON
(G) HEPTAGON

NOW CHECK YOUR ANSWERS AND KEEP A RECORD OF YOUR SCORE.

1 A (SCORE 1 POINT).

In each row, the first symbol is the same as the second in the previous row, and the other symbols continue in the same order.

2 2 (SCORE 1 POINT).

The first column totals 9. The second column totals 10. This pattern continues, so the final column should total 13, by the addition of 2.

3 J (SCORE 1 POINT).

The word is: ADJUST. (Datsun is not allowed.)

4 (A) (SCORE 1 POINT).

An anagram of HORSE. All the others are anagrams of fish:
(B) PIKE
(C) TROUT
(D) BASS

5 L (SCORE 1 POINT).

The block (the black portion) should be on the right of the letter.

6 SEPTEMBER (SCORE 1 POINT).

These are the number of days in the months. September is the only month which has two 31-day months before it and one after it.

7 (B) (SCORE 1 POINT).

All other words contain AMEN.

8 (SCORE 1 POINT IF ALL ARE CORRECT; ½ POINT IF 5 ARE CORRECT.)
(A) maCHINe
(B) alLEGro
(C) wHEELbarrow
(D) deLIVERy
(E) sHIPmate
(F) alARM

9 ag ci bf dk ej hl (SCORE 1 POINT).

10 21 (SCORE 1 POINT).

The numbers increase by 3, 4, 5, 6, and 7.

11 (SCORE 1 POINT IF ALL ARE CORRECT; ½ POINT IF 8 OR 9 ARE CORRECT.)

asteriSK	ALimoNY
SKaTE	NYION
TErminUS	ONsET
USaGE	ETymologiST
GEnerAL	STreet

12 G and H (SCORE 1 POINT).

13 LIME (SCORE 1 POINT).

The words are:
aliment
sublime
limerick

14 X is 4; Y is 11 (SCORE 1 POINT IF BOTH ARE CORRECT).

Two alternate series
Starting with the first number: 7   6   5   4   3
Starting with the second number: 8   9   10   11   12

15 (SCORE 1 POINT IF ALL ARE CORRECT; ½ POINT IF 6 ARE CORRECT.)
(E) TETRAGON — 4 sides
(C) PENTAGON — 5 sides
(B) HEXAGON — 6 sides
(G) HEPTAGON — 7 sides
(A) OCTAGON — 8 sides
(F) NONAGON — 9 sides
(D) DECAGON — 10 sides

Record your score.

NOW TOTAL UP YOUR SCORES FOR THE FIRST FOUR TESTS AND COMPARE THEM WITH THE RATINGS THAT FOLLOW.

NOTES

Two of the problems—8 and 11—require fairly long written answers (allowed for in the time limit).

The volunteers experienced most difficulty with 8, 11, and 15.

RATINGS IN GROUP I

TEST 1	Average 8½ points
TEST 2	Average 7½ points
TEST 3	Average 10 points
TEST 4	Average 9 points

TOTAL FOR THE GROUP

Out of a possible 60 points:

Over 52	Excellent
46–52	Very good
36–45	Good
35	Average
30–34	Fair
Under 30	Poor

Especially if you scored 26 or under, it is suggested that you go through the problems again, in conjunction with the answers and explanations, so that you will have a better understanding of the tests to follow.

GROUP II

CHALLENGING LEVEL

1 Solve the clues, and two boys' names will appear in the vertical columns headed **x** and **y**.

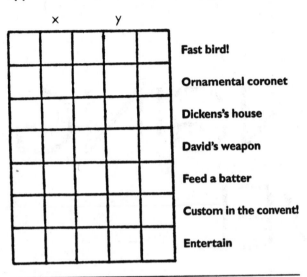

Fast bird!

Ornamental coronet

Dickens's house

David's weapon

Feed a batter

Custom in the convent!

Entertain

2 Which triangle is wrong?

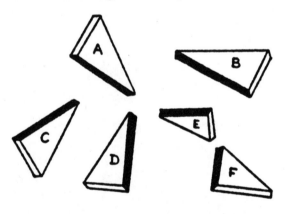

3 Square the third-lowest even number and subtract the result from the third-highest odd number:

9	67	4	11	58	66
2	65	1	8	10	41
6	71	5	12	25	3
7	41	32	70	69	68

4 Which is the odd one out?

(A) FEDERATION
(B) OUTSPAN
(C) CANOPY
(D) COUPON
(D) ABUTS
(F) REDCAP

5 What should go into the empty segment?

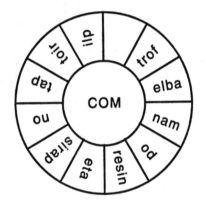

6 Whose face is in the mirror?

7 What is X?

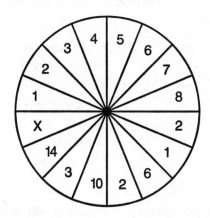

---

8 TWO different words can be made by inserting two different letters into the blank space. You must give both words.

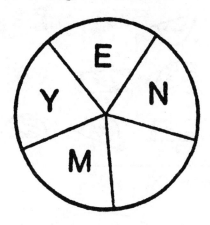

9 Which words go into the brackets? Each word must logically follow the previous word and precede the next word, e.g., putting (GREEN) land.

COMMON
(A) (　　　)
KICK
(B) (　　　)
PIPE
(C) (　　　)
BACK
(D) (　　　)
STATION
(E) (　　　)
PIECE
(F) (　　　)
TIME
(G) (　　　)
SPOON
(H) (　　　)
STOCK
(I) (　　　)
WISE
(J) (　　　)
DOWN

10 Which of the numbered circles at the bottom should be placed at A, B, C, and D?

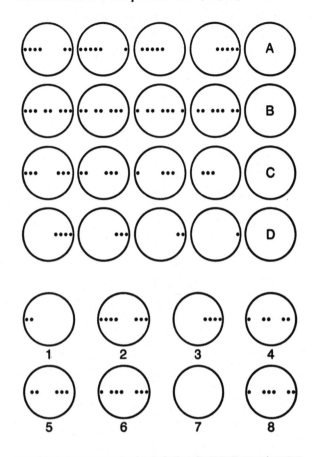

11 What is the difference between the lowest number and the average of all the numbers?

3   9   12   15   18   25   30

12 Here are seven common words. Which is the odd one out?

(A) DIM
(B) MIND
(C) MILL
(D) LIVID
(E) VIM
(F) MIX
(G) CIVIL

13 Give words to fit the definitions. Each word removes one letter from the word above it.

- - - - - - -	Place for cigarettes
- - - - - -	Not on the right course
- - - - -	Go off course
- - - -	Shallow vessel
- - -	Sea-fish
- -	Affirmative
-	Musical note

14 Which three pieces below will make the face above?

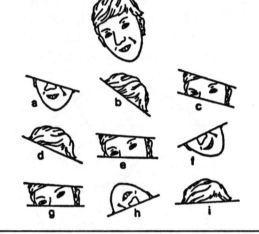

15 What is X?

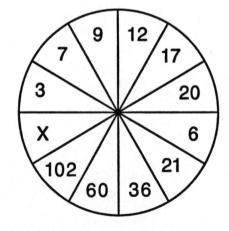

NOW CHECK YOUR ANSWERS AND KEEP A RECORD OF YOUR SCORE.

1 X is WILLIAM; Y is FRANCIS (SCORE 1 POINT IF BOTH ARE CORRECT.)

s	W	i	F	t
t	I	a	R	a
b	L	e	A	k
s	L	i	N	g
p	I	t	C	h
h	A	b	I	t
a	M	u	S	e

2 F (SCORE 1 POINT).

The shorter side is shaded. In all the other triangles the longer side is shaded.

3 31 (SCORE 1 POINT).

4 (C) (SCORE 1 POINT).

CANOPY contains three consecutive letters in their correct order. All the other words contain three consecutive letters in reverse order.

5 TNA (SCORE 1 POINT).

Each word starts with COM.

The syllables that follow are read backwards in the outer sections:

COM - FORT - ABLE
COM - MAN - DO
COM - MISER - ATE
COM - PARIS - ON
COM - PAT - RIOT
COM - PLI - ANT

6 A (SCORE 1 POINT).

7 4 (SCORE 1 POINT).

Moving clockwise and starting with number 1 in the upper half, compare each number with that in its opposite segment. 1 is doubled, giving 2 in the opposite segment; the next number (2) is halved, giving 1 in the opposite segment. The same procedure continues: double the next, then halve the next.

8 in the upper half is halved to give 4 in the opposite segment.

(An alternative solution is to double all the odd numbers and halve all the even numbers).

8 E (ENEMY) and O (MONEY) (SCORE 1 POINT IF BOTH ARE CORRECT).

9 (SCORE 1 POINT IF ALL ARE CORRECT; ½ POINT IF 8 OR 9 ARE CORRECT.)

(A) PLACE		(F) MEAL	
(B) STAND		(G) TABLE	
(C) LINE		(H) FEED	
(D) FIRE		(I) MARKET	
(E) MASTER		(J) CRACK	

10 A 3; B 6; C 1; D 7 (SCORE 1 POINT IF ALL ARE CORRECT; ½ POINT IF 3 ARE CORRECT.)

Careful examination of the spots indicates the direction of rotation.

The first row rotates from left to right; the second row rotates from right to left; the third row rotates from right to left; the fourth row rotates from left to right.

11 13 (SCORE 1 POINT).

12 (B) (SCORE 1 POINT).

All the other words are made up of Roman numerals. N is not a Roman numeral.

13 (SCORE 1 POINT IF ALL ARE CORRECT.)

ASHTRAY
ASTRAY
STRAY
TRAY
RAY
AY
A

14 b, e, and h (SCORE 1 POINT IF ALL ARE CORRECT).

15 140 (SCORE 1 POINT).

Starting with 3 in the upper half, the number in the opposite segment multiplies it by 2. The next number (7) is multiplied by 3; then by 4, and so on. Therefore, 20 is multiplied by 7 to give 140.

Remember to record your score.

NOTES

In question number 6, the volunteers did not always realize that the stripes in the tie are diagonally reversed in a mirror reflection.

Numbers 7 and 15 seemed to give the greatest difficulty, though much time was lost (not always to produce a successful result) on number 9.

1 Which cup is the odd one out?

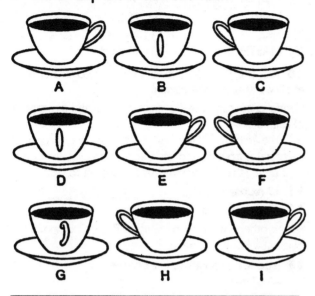

2 What is the TOTAL number of spots on the rear side?

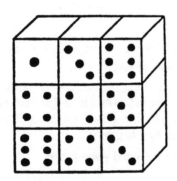

3 The same four letters in a different order will complete these words:

(A) ----t e d
(B) l ----
(C) ----t
(D) e y ----l
(E) c u l p ----

4 What comes next?

124   81   6   32   641   2   -

5 Which is the odd one out?

(A) HEARD   (D) URCHIN
(B) RUSHING   (E) DIAGNOSED
(C) CLIPPER   (F) MONEYED

6 What are a, b, c, and d?

3	27	1	32	4	26	3	29
5	25	5	26	6	a	b	c	d

7 What letter should go into the empty space?

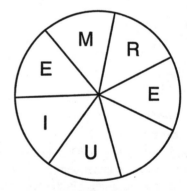

8 What letters should be substituted for X and Y on the last cube?

9 If this shape were folded along the dotted lines, it could be made into a cube:

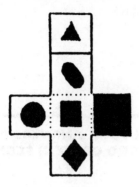

like this:

If this cube were turned upside-down, which of these faces would appear at the top?

A   **B**   **C**

---

10 What are x, y, and z?

```
A  I   3    L  12   6    M  13   9
0  15  12   S  19   x    y   z
```

---

11 The same word can precede each of these word-endings:

(A) CASS
(B) BON
(C) TON
(D) GO
(E) EEN

---

12 Examine the first three car license plates and then complete the last one:

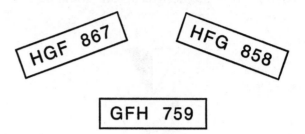

GFH 759

FGH

---

13 What are x, y, and z?

3	42	40
7	52	53
12	63	68
18	75	85
25	88	104
X	102	125
42	Y	148
52	133	Z

14 If this design were turned ninety degrees counter-clockwise and held in front of a mirror, which of the designs below would be reflected?

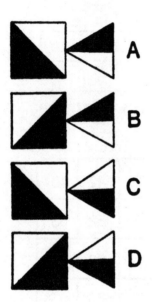

A

B

C

D

15 All of these might be found in a subway station, but you must unscramble them first:

(A) KENERKLOCTO
(B) PRAMLOFT
(C) LETISRUNT
(D) TORDUCNOC
(E) SEXPRES

NOW CHECK YOUR ANSWERS AND KEEP A RECORD OF YOUR SCORE.

1 G (SCORE 1 POINT).
The handle is in the wrong position as compared with B and D.

2 29 (SCORE 1 POINT).
Opposite faces of a die add up to 7. Therefore, moving horizontally from left to right and starting in the top row, opposite faces are: 6 4 1 3 5 2 1 3 4

3 B A L E (in any order) (SCORE 1 POINT IF ALL ARE CORRECT; ½ POINT IF 4 ARE CORRECT.)
The words become:
(A) BELATED
(B) LABEL
(C) BLEAT
(D) EYEBALL
(E) CULPABLE

4 8 (SCORE 1 POINT).
This is an ordinary "doubling" series, but incorrectly spaced. When correctly spaced, the answer becomes obvious: 1 2 4 8 16 32 64 128

5 (B) (SCORE 1 POINT).
This contains SHIN - part of the leg. All the others contain parts of the head or face:
(A) HEARD - contains EAR
(C) CLIPPER - contains LIP
(D) URCHIN - contains CHIN
(E) DIAGNOSED - contains NOSE
(F) MONEYED - contains EYE

6 a is 24; b is 7; c is 23; d is 7 (SCORE 1 POINT IF ALL ARE CORRECT; ½ POINT IF 2 OR 3 ARE CORRECT).
There are four series. Starting with the first term and taking every fourth term thereafter:
3 4 5 6 7(d)
Starting with the second term and continuing in the same way:
27 26 25 24(a)
Starting with the third term:
1 3 5 7(b)
Starting with the fourth term:
32 29 26 23(c)

7 Q (SCORE 1 POINT).
The word is REQUIEM.

8 X is I, Y is Q (SCORE 1 POINT IF BOTH ARE CORRECT; ½ POINT IF ONE IS CORRECT.)
The front face of each cube advances the letter on the right face by four positions in the alphabet. The top face advances the front face by three positions on the first cube, then by four positions, then by five positions, and so on. (Alternatively: increase the top faces by 7 positions at a time, the other faces by 6 positions at a time).

9 C (SCORE 1 POINT).

10 x is 15; y is T; z is 20 (SCORE 1 POINT IF ALL ARE CORRECT; ½ POINT IF 2 ARE CORRECT).
There are three series.
Starting with the first term and taking every third term thereafter:
A L M O S—The only letter that will complete a word is T (ALMOST)—represented by y. The number that follows each letter represents the position in the alphabet of that letter. Therefore, T—represented by y—should be followed by 20 (T is the 20th letter)—the value for z.
Starting with the third term and taking every third term thereafter: 3 6 9 12 15 (the value for x).

11 CAR (SCORE 1 POINT).
The words become:
(A) CARCASS
(B) CARBON
(C) CARTON
(D) CARGO
(E) CAREEN

12 669 (SCORE 1 POINT).
The first three license plates follow the same pattern.
The first letter gives the first digit (H is 8—its position in the alphabet).
The second letter gives the second digit by reducing its alphabetical position by 1 (G—the 7th letter—becomes 6).
The third letter gives the third digit by increasing its alphabetical position by 1 (F becomes 7, increasing its 6th position by 1).
Therefore, in the final license plate:
F gives 6 (the 6th letter)
G gives 6 (reducing the 7th letter by one)
H gives 9 (increasing the 8th letter by one).

13 x is 33; y is 117; z is 173 (SCORE 1 POINT IF ALL ARE
CORRECT; ½ POINT IF 2 ARE CORRECT).

Moving down the left-hand vertical column, the numbers increase by 4, 5, 6, and so on. 25 should be
increased by 8 to give 33—the value for x.

The middle vertical column increases by 10, 11, 12,
and so on. 102 should be increased by 15 to give 117—
the value for y.

The right-hand vertical column increases progres-
sively—13, 15, 17, 19, and so on. 148 should be
increased by 25 to give 173—the value for z.

14 A (SCORE 1 POINT).

15 (SCORE 1 POINT IF ALL ARE CORRECT; ½ POINT IF 4
ARE CORRECT.)

(A) TOKEN CLERK
(B) PLATFORM
(C) TURNSTILE
(D) CONDUCTOR
(E) EXPRESS

Remember to record your score.

NOTES

Definitely the most difficult test so far, this one pro-
duced very low scores by the volunteers.

Questions 6 and 10 gave examples of the "multiple
series" type of question, that is, two or more series
embraced in an overall series, where every second,
third, or fourth term has to be considered. It is good
to become accustomed to this type of question since
the same principle may be repeated in later tests.

Number 4 is an example of a simple series incorrectly
spaced. Again, you may come across similar problems
later.

Questions 4, 6, 8, and 12 gave the greatest difficulty.
The time limit was extended to compensate for the
test's complexity.

1 Which is the odd one out?

(A) IAMBUS   (D) PAEON
(B) TROCHEE   (E) SPONDEE
(C) RONDURE   (F) DACTYL

2 Which one is different?

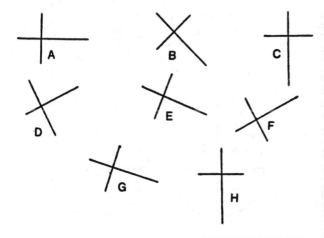

3 What comes next in the series?

16   72   38   94   50   -

4 The black ball moves one position at a time clockwise. The white ball moves two positions at a time counter-clockwise.
a) In how many moves will they be together again?
b) In which corner will they be when they meet?

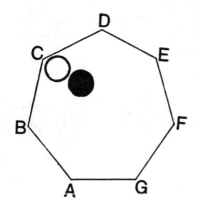

5 What is X?

1	2	3	4	5	6	7	8
7	14	1	2	2	1	8	7
10	3	4	18	2	1	8	6
8	5	11	12	2	21	3	4
2	11	6	3	13	1	2	10
2	5	5	1	6	10	2	X

6 A sentence may conceal a "hidden" word. Thus, in this sentence the word ENSIGN is "hidden": HeathENS IGNore Christians. What "voices" are hidden in these sentences?

(A) "Parsifal," set to music, is very popular.
(B) Mr. Allsop ran on to win the race.
(C) They often organize concerts.
(D) Rumbas, sambas, and waltzes are my favorite dances.
(E) The total tonnage is ten thousand.

7 If the two dotted lines are placed together, what will be the result?

35

8 What are x and y?

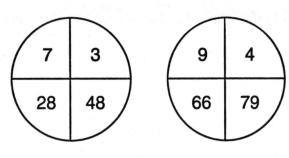

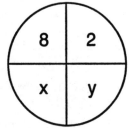

9 Arrange these in order of length, starting with the shortest:

(A) DECAMETER　　(E) DECIMETER
(B) CENTIMETER　　(F) METER
(C) MILLIMETER　　(G) HECTOMETER
(D) KILOMETER

10 Which flag is wrong—and WHY?

11 Who is the odd man out?

(A) MARCONI　　(D) BAIRD
(B) CARUSO　　(E) WHITNEY
(C) EDISON

12 What are x and y?

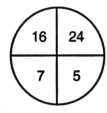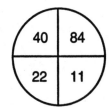

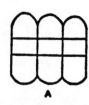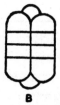

13 Which is the odd one out?

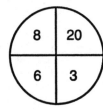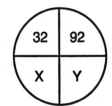

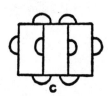

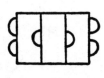

14 What comes next in this series?

1072   1055   1021   953   817   545   -

---

15 Complete the final square:

935	824	713
148	365	582

KWG	JVF	IUE
UAM	WCJ	YEG

X7Z	W6Y	
3U7	5W4	

NOW CHECK YOUR ANSWERS AND
KEEP A RECORD OF YOUR SCORE.

1 (C) (SCORE I POINT).

RONDURE is a round outline or object.

All the others are metrical feet:

(A) IAMBUS: a short accent followed by a long one;

(B) TROCHEE: a long accent followed by a short one;

(D) PAEON: a long accent (placed anywhere) and three short ones;

(E) SPONDEE: two long accents;

(F) DACTYL: a long accent followed by two short ones.

2 D (SCORE I POINT).

The lines are of equal length. In all the others, one line is longer (or shorter) than the other.

3 16 (SCORE I POINT).

Each number reverses the previous number and adds 1 to each digit. Thus, in the first two terms, 16 reversed is 61, which then changes to 72. In the final term, 50 reversed becomes 05, which in turn becomes 16 by adding one to each digit.

4 (A) 7; (B) C (SCORE I POINT IF BOTH ARE CORRECT; ½ POINT IF ONE IS CORRECT).

	Black Ball	White Ball
1st move	D	A
2nd move	E	F
3rd move	F	D
4th move	G	B
5th move	A	G
6th move	B	E
7th move	C	C

5 5 (SCORE I POINT).

Columns headed by an odd number add up to 30. Columns headed by an even number add up to 40. The last column adds up to 35, to which must be added 5 to bring it up to 40, as this column is headed by an even number.

6 (SCORE I POINT IF ALL ARE CORRECT; ½ POINT IF 4 ARE CORRECT.)

(A) FALSETTO

(B) SOPRANO

(C) TENOR

(D) BASS

(E) ALTO

7 THEME (SCORE I POINT).

This is the result of placing them together:

8 x is 11; y is 61 (SCORE I POINT IF BOTH ARE CORRECT; ½ POINT IF ONE IS CORRECT).

In the first circle, the number in the top left quarter is squared and then reduced by 1 in the opposite diagonal quarter; the number in the top right quarter is cubed and then 1 added to give the number in the opposite lower quarter.

In the second circle the same procedure is followed, except that 2 is deducted from the squared number and 2 is added to the cubed number.

Therefore, in the third circle, 3 is deducted from the square of 8 (64 becomes 61, the value for y), while 3 is added to the cube of 2 (8 becomes 11, the value for x).

9 (SCORE I POINT IF ALL ARE CORRECT; ½ POINT IF 6 ARE CORRECT.)

(C) MILLIMETER

(B) CENTIMETER

(E) DECIMETER

(F) METER

(A) DECAMETER

(G) HECTOMETER

(D) KILOMETER

10 (B) (SCORE I POINT). The stripes should alternate from the edge of the flag, dark–light. In (B) they begin light–dark.

11 (B) (SCORE I POINT). Caruso was a singer. All the others were inventors.

12 x is 9 or 24; y is also 9 or 24 (SCORE I POINT IF BOTH ARE CORRECT).

In each case, the numbers at the top are divided by 4 in the opposite quarter and 1 is added.

An alternative solution is that the numbers in the lower quarters are multiplied by 4 in their opposite quarters and 4 is deducted from the result.

13 C **(SCORE I POINT).**

In C there are 8 curves and 6 straight lines. In all the others there are 6 curves and 6 straight lines.

14 I **(SCORE I POINT).**

The numbers reduce by 17, 34, 68, 136, 272, and so on—544 therefore reduces the previous number 545 by 1. (The terms reduce in multiples of 17.)

15 **(SCORE I POINT.)**

In the top line, all the way through, whether using letters or numbers, they reduce by one position in each successive square.

In the bottom line, they increase by two positions, except for the last term, which reduces its position by three places from that in the previous square.

Remember to record your score.

NOTES

The numerical problems seemed to give our volunteers the greatest difficulty—3, 5, and 14 particularly, though 5 was based more on logical thinking than on the numbers themselves.

Few succeeded with question number I and, surprisingly (now that the metric system has become more mainstream), number 9 caused a lot of problems, even though (B), (C), (F), and (D) were correctly placed.

(You may rest after 25 minutes and then continue for another 20 minutes.)

1 What is x?

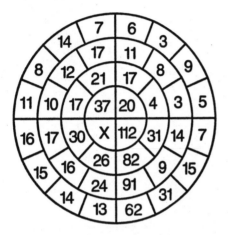

2 Which one is wrong?

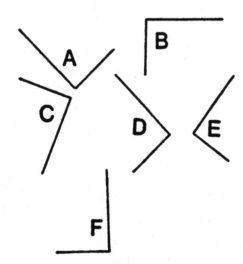

3 Which of the figures at the bottom should follow the six figures at the top?

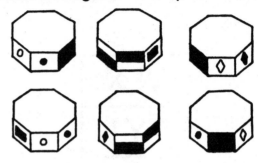

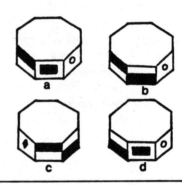

4 What comes next in this series?

I III VI X XV XXI XXVIII -

5 Complete this crossword puzzle, choosing words from the list below:

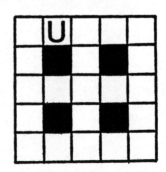

TULIP
BURST
QUEST
EAGLE
RATIO
FULLY
LEVER
ANGER
QUART
TORCH
TEETH

6 Which is the odd one out?

(A) ESOPHAGUS   (D) STERNUM
(B) SCAPULA   (E) ULNA
(C) CLAVICLE   (F) HUMERUS

---

7 17 is to 101
as 13 is to 77,
and as 19 is to __?

---

8 Join these words to form 10 other words or word pairs.

TEN	DEN	ORC	MATE	LIGHT
SCHOOL	SUN	HOME	HID	DON
WAY	DAY	HIGH	KEY	BOY
BULB	MON	LAND	HARD	CHECK

---

9 Which currency belongs to which country?

(A) KRONE   (1) SPAIN
(B) LIRA   (2) DENMARK
(C) PESETA   (3) PORTUGAL
(D) ESCUDO   (4) RUSSIA
(E) RUBLE   (5) ITALY

10

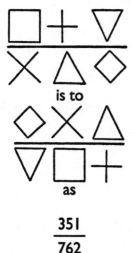

is to

$$\frac{351}{762}$$

is to
?

---

11 What comes next in this series?

1	0	11	E	8	E	12	T
	2	T	3	T	4	-	

---

12 All of these shapes—except one—are of the same area. Which is the exception, and is it of greater or lesser area?

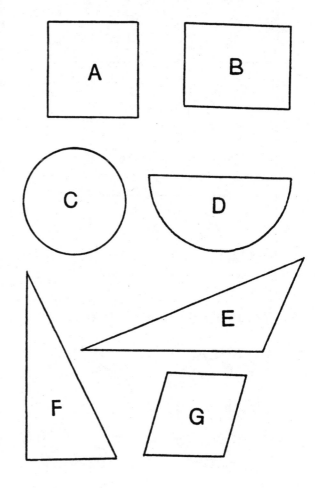

13 Which of these is wrong?

A
> "A thing of beauty
> is a joy for ever."
>
> John Keats, 1795-1821

B
> "If you can keep your head
> when all about you/Are
> losing theirs…"
>
> Rudyard Kipling, 1865-1936

C
> "My heart's in the
> the Highlands, my
> heart is not here."
>
> Robert Burns, 1739-1796

D
> "If music be the food
> of love, play on."
>
> William Shakespeare, 1564-1616

14 What does the third clock show?

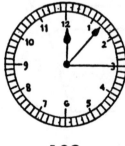

LOG

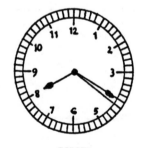

HUT

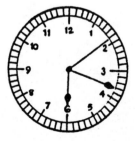

15 Which number is nearest to the number which is midway between the lowest and the highest number?

11	84	41	9	79
81	7	36	51	47
88	12	8	89	10

NOW CHECK YOUR ANSWERS AND KEEP A RECORD OF YOUR SCORE.

42

1 55 (SCORE I POINT).

In each quarter, add the numbers in the outer ring, then those in the next ring, and then the next.

In the top left quarter these totals descend:

40 39 38 37   (the single number in the center).

In the top right quarter they descend:

23 22 21 20   (the single number in the center).

In the right lower quarter they descend:

115 114 113 112   (the single number in the center).

Therefore, in the lower left quarter they descend:

58 57 56   and then, obviously, 55 (x).

2 E (SCORE I POINT).

Both lines are shorter than those in the other angles.

3 a (SCORE I POINT).

The figure is rotating counter-clockwise, three faces at a time. The designs on the respective faces can be discovered by examining the figures at the top, which are in this sequence:

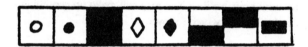

4 XXXVI (SCORE I POINT).

First change the Roman numerals into modern numerals:

1   3   6   10   15   21   28

It can be seen that the terms increase by:

2, 3, 4, 5, 6, and 7.

Therefore, the final number must increase the previous one by 8 (28 increases to 36, or XXXVI in Roman numerals).

5 EITHER OF THESE SOLUTIONS SCORES I POINT.

6 (A) (SCORE I POINT).

ESOPHAGUS is the canal from the mouth to the stomach. All the others are bones:

(B) SCAPULA—shoulder blade

(C) CLAVICLE—collarbone

(D) STERNUM—breastbone

(E) ULNA—inner bone of the forearm

(F) HUMERUS—bone of the upper arm

7 113 (SCORE I POINT).

In each case, the number is multiplied by 6 and 1 is subtracted from the result.

8 (SCORE I POINT IF ALL ARE CORRECT; ½ POINT IF 8 OR 9 ARE CORRECT.)

TEN	DON
MON	KEY
ORC	HARD
HID	DEN
SUN	DAY
LIGHT	BULB
CHECK	MATE
HOME	LAND
HIGH	WAY
SCHOOL	BOY

9 (A) (2); (B) (5); (C) (1); (D) (3); (E) (4) (SCORE I POINT IF ALL ARE CORRECT).

10 (SCORE I POINT.)

$$\frac{276}{135}$$

11 F (SCORE I POINT).

Each letter is the initial letter of the previous number, therefore:

4 (FOUR) is followed by F.

12 G is of LESSER area than the others, which are all of the same area (SCORE I POINT).

13 C (SCORE I POINT).

The definite article (THE) is repeated in the second line.

14 FIR (SCORE I POINT).

The first letter is indicated by the position of the hour hand relative to the hours—in this case 6, that is, the sixth letter (F).

The next letter is shown by the position of the second hand. Here it is on the ninth second, and the ninth letter is I.

The third letter is indicated by the position of the minute hand. As it points to the eighteenth minute, it shows that the letter is R—the eighteenth letter in the alphabet.

15 36 (SCORE I POINT).

Record your score.

NOW TOTAL UP YOUR SCORES FOR THE FOUR TESTS AND COMPARE THEM WITH THE RATINGS THAT FOLLOW.

NOTES

This was a difficult test for our volunteers.

Questions 1, 2, 4, and 9 gained the most correct answers, but 3 and 5 might have, had they really puzzled.

In 13, it was surprisingly easy to overlook the fact that the definite article was repeated. When a book (such as this!) is in the proof stage, before being printed, it is the job of the proofreader to spot any solecisms—which creep in insidiously, however careful the typesetter has been. Proofreading is itself a very specialized job, and yet, surprisingly, it is easy enough to overlook a printing error like the one in question 13.

RATINGS IN GROUP II

TEST I	Average 7 points
TEST 2	Average 5 1/2 points
TEST 3	Average 8 points
TEST 4	Average 5 1/2 points

TOTAL FOR THE GROUP

Out of a possible 60 points:

Over 48	Excellent
40–47	Very good
27–39	Good
26	Average
20–25	Fair
Under 20	Poor

Although most of these problems were more difficult than those in the previous group, a score under 20 implies that you should try to acquire a better understanding of these types of tests. It would be a good idea to retry all the problems up to here, in conjunction with the answers. As the final ratings—given at the end of all three groups—are the important ones for assessing your IQ, do not lose heart if your scores up until now are low. You may still make up ground in the final group which follows.

GROUP III

MASTERFUL LEVEL

(You may rest after 45 minutes and then continue for another 30 minutes.)

1 Complete these words, using all the letters contained in this grammatically incorrect sentence:

HERE IS TEN FAT CATTLE
(A) - E - R - S - M - N -
(B) - R - N - P - R - N -
(C) - O - T - N- N - A -

2 Which of the lower circles should take the place of number 5?

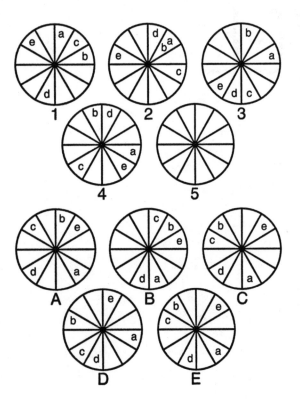

3 When a dart lands in an even number, the next throw lands it in the second odd number clockwise.

When a dart lands in an odd number, the next throw lands it in the third even number clockwise from the previous throw.

As you can see, the first dart has already been thrown.

Four more darts are to be thrown. What will be the total score of the five darts?

4 Using the top card sequence as a key, what famous author is this?

5 What letter starts the last word?

PATCH
KINK
TEAS
—END

6 A clock shows 9:25. If it were held upside-down in front of a mirror, which of those below would be reflected?

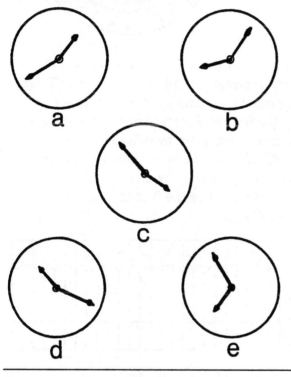

a

b

c

d

e

7 Which number in the bottom line should come next in the top line?

15 16 21 20 9 88 18 28 -
7 34 19 17 22 66

8 Find the words for A, B, C, D, E, F, G, and H:

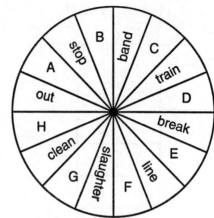

9 Which is the odd one out?

(A) USDA
(B) NATO
(C) NASA
(D) KIWI
(E) NAFTA

10 The top band rotates counter-clockwise.
The middle band rotates clockwise.
The bottom band rotates counter-clockwise.

Each movement brings the next number into position, and there are eight numbers on each band, continuing in the same order on the hidden sides.

After 7 moves, what will be the sum of the three numbers in the vertical column above A, and also the sum of the three numbers above B?

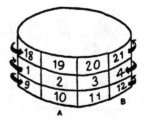

11 What comes next here?

1 8 2 7 6 4 1 2 5 2 1 -

12 What is X?

T	0
18	B
O	5
7	M
H	12
19	A
X	2

13 Which of the numbered figures at the bottom should take the places of A, B, and C?

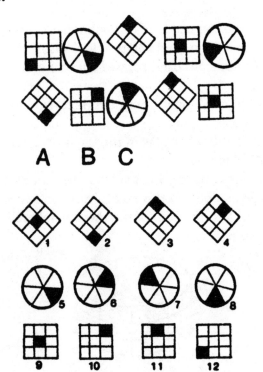

14 What is X?

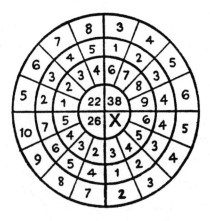

15 A advances 1 place, then 2, then 3, etc., increasing its jump by one each time.

B advances 2 places, then 3, then 4, etc., increasing its jump by one each time.

C advances 3 places, then 4, then 5, etc., increasing its jump by one each time.

Which will be the first to reach 25 EXACTLY?

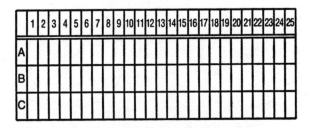

NOW CHECK YOUR ANSWERS AND KEEP A RECORD OF YOUR SCORE.

1 (SCORE 1 POINT IF ALL ARE CORRECT.)

(A) REFRESHMENT

(B) TRANSPARENT

(C) CONTINENTAL

2 E (SCORE 1 POINT).

a moves one place at a time clockwise,

b moves one place at a time counter-clockwise,

c moves two places at a time clockwise;

d moves to and from opposite segments;

e moves counter-clockwise, first one place, then two, then three, and so on.

3 68 (SCORE 1 POINT)

1st throw ... 18

2nd throw ... 15

3rd throw ... 8

4th throw ... 9

5th throw ... 18 (again)

Total 68

4 MARK TWAIN (SCORE 1 POINT).

The four cards at the top indicate the first 23 letters of the alphabet.

Ace of hearts up to the 5 ... 1-5, or A to E

Ace of clubs up to the 4 ... 6-9, F to I

Ace of spades up to the 7 ... 10-16, or J to P

Ace of diamonds up to the 7 ... 17-23, or Q to W

5 V (SCORE 1 POINT).

Giving each letter a value according to its position in the alphabet, each word must have a total letter-value of 45.

The three letters of the unfinished word have a total of 23, which must be increased to 45 with the addition of 22—that is, the 22nd letter of the alphabet—V.

6 b (SCORE 1 POINT).

7 66 (SCORE 1 POINT).

The numbers at the top are divisible by 3 and 4 alternately.

The only number in the bottom line that is divisible by 3 is 66.

8 (SCORE 1 POINT IF ALL CORRECT; ½ POINT IF 7 ARE CORRECT.)

The position of the letters from A to H indicates that the words are considered in a clockwise direction. Starting with OUT, and reading clockwise:

    out

(A) BACK

    stop

(B) WATCH

    band

(C) WAGON

    train

(D) STATION

    break

(E) FRONT

    line

(F) MAN

    slaughter

(G) HOUSE

    clean

(H) CUT

    out

9 (D) (SCORE 1 POINT).

Apart from KIWI, which is a non-flying bird, a fruit, and also a slang term for a non-flying member of the New Zealand Air Force, the others are all acronyms (words formed from the initial letters of other words):

(A) USDA   United States Department of Agriculture

(B) NATO   North Atlantic Treaty Organization

(C) NASA   National Aeronautic and Space Administration

(E) NAFTA North American Free Trade Agreement

10 A 32; B 38 (SCORE 1 POINT IF BOTH ARE CORRECT; ½ POINT IF 1 IS CORRECT).

	A	B
1st move	18	20
	3	5
	9	11
2nd move	25	19
	4	6
	16	10
3rd move	24	18
	5	7
	15	9

4th move	23	25
	6	8
	14	16
5th move	22	24
	7	1
	13	15
6th move	21	23
	8	2
	12	14
7th move	20	22
	1	3
	11	13
Total	32	38

11 6 (SCORE 1 POINT).

Correcting the spacing, the series becomes:

1   8   27   64   125   21   -

That is: the cubes of: 1, 2, 3, 4, 5, 6. The cube of 6 is 216, which means that 6 must follow 21.

12 R (SCORE 1 POINT).

Substituting numbers for letters according to their position in the alphabet, each horizontal row adds up to 20. Therefore, X must be 18, as it is paired with 2, and R is the 18th letter.

13 A 5; B 2; C 12 (SCORE 1 POINT IF ALL ARE CORRECT; ½ POINT IF 2 ARE CORRECT).

Consider the movements of the black section in each figure. It goes diagonally across the square from bottom left to top right and then back again:

In the circle, it moves two segments at a time in a clockwise direction:

In the diamond it moves alternately from top to bottom:

14 22 (SCORE 1 POINT).

In each quarter of the circle:

add the numbers in the outer ring; subtract the sum of the numbers in the next ring; add the sum of the numbers in the next ring to give the number that goes into the inner section. So:

the sum of 2, 3, 4, and 5 14
subtract the sum of 1, 2, 3, and 4 . . .10
$$\overline{4}$$
add the sum of 3, 4, 5, and 6 18
$$\overline{22}$$

15 C (SCORE 1 POINT).

The relative positions are shown below:

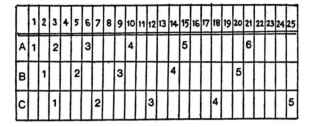

Remember to record your score.

NOTES

Questions 4, 7, 8, 10, and 13 were probably the most difficult. Regarding 4 (since you may come across other problems of this kind), it is worth bearing in mind the coincidence that there are 52 cards in a pack—or 26 in half a pack (the equivalent of two suits)—and 26 letters in the alphabet. Be aware of this fact, as we may use this tactic again in the future.

I was amused to witness the antics of some volunteers who were trying to figure out the answer to number 6. Holding the page upside-down, and even holding it up to the light and trying to see through it from the reverse side were common strategies.

As for number 11, you were advised previously to keep an eye open for series—such as this—which were incorrectly spaced. I hope that you benefited from past experience.

(You may rest after 30 minutes and then continue for another 30 minutes.)

I Which of the numbered arrows belongs to X?

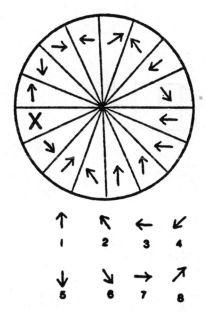

2 What goes into the last rectangle?

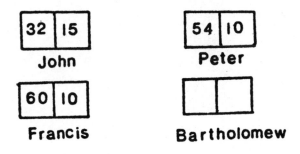

3 Pinion (gear wheel) A is the driving pinion, while pinion B idles on its stub axle.

The black teeth of these pinions are meshed with teeth in the outer ring.
(A) After four revolutions of A in a counter-clockwise direction, where will the black tooth of pinion B be?
(B) And where will it be when A has revolved clockwise through one revolution and then to where the tooth marked x meshes with the outer ring?

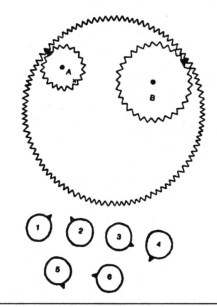

4 Which of the numbers in the bottom line should be placed under 17 in the top line?

2	3	4	5	6	7	8	10	11	17
7	2	17	6	13	8	3	5	4	

9   15   20   33   21   25

5 What comes next in this series?

I	S	I	T	P	N	A	A
D	L	I	I	Y	N	-	

---

6 Supply words to go into the brackets. Each word must link logically with the preceding word and the following word, e.g., tea (POT) roast.

FOOD
(   )
LETTER
(   )
STRONG
(   )
STRING
(   )
BAG
(   )
BOMB
(   )
SHOCK
(   )
LENGTH
(   )
CRACK

7 Imagine that blocks x and y are removed from the arrangement below, and that the remaining shape is turned upside-down.
Which of the other shapes will result?

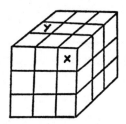

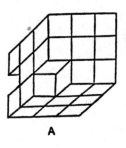

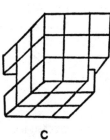

A

B

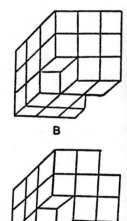

C

D

8 These clocks are all wrong, as indicated. If they are all correctly adjusted, which clock will show the time nearest to 12 o'clock?

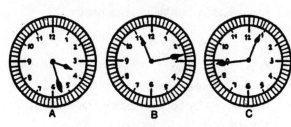

A	B	C
2¼ hours fast	1 hour slow	1 hour 20 minutes fast

9

 = 3 6 6

 = 3 8 10

 = 5 6 0

 = ?

10 What comes next?

2 3 4 6 1 2 2 0
1 8 4 8 1 0 –

11 Discover the key from these three problems and then break this NAVAL code.

1	2		6	8		2	1
3	4					2	2
4	9		5	2		1	3
						1	1
A	B		T	E		E	S

12 Which is the odd one out?

(A) OUTSTRIP
(B) RED CURRANT
(C) SIGHING
(D) SELF-EDUCATED
(E) BIG FEET
(F) IRONMAN

13 Without using a pocket calculator, which of these investments would give the greatest interest?

(A) $1,000 at 5% simple interest for 4 years;
(B) $700 at 8% compound interest for 3 years;
(C) $900 at 7% simple interest for 3 years;
(D) $800 at 6% compound interest for 4 years.

---

14 Give values for A, B, and C:

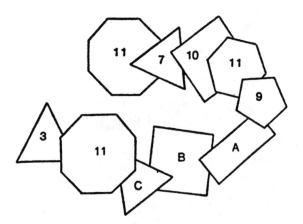

15 Write the words that fit these definitions in the corresponding rows below:

1 No lover of foreigners.
2 Remove objectionable reading matter.
3 Stuffing art!
4 Still valid.
5 Not liable for duty.
6 Hydrogen and oxygen.
7 Headwear—for holding medical preparations?
8 Correct on religious doctrines.
9 It receives the mail.

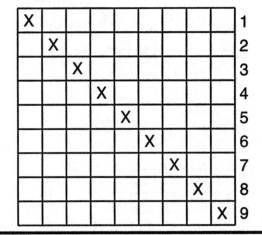

NOW CHECK YOUR ANSWERS AND KEEP A RECORD OF YOUR SCORE.

1 4 (SCORE 1 POINT).
Start with the arrow above X. In the opposite segment it is turned 90 degrees counter-clockwise. The next is turned 90 degrees clockwise. This alternating rotation is continued. Therefore, in the opposite segment to X, the arrow must be turned 90 degrees clockwise (number 4).

2 (SCORE 1 POINT IF CORRECT.)
96 36
Add the letter-values of the consonants according to their position in the alphabet and enter the total in the left-hand side.
     Then enter the total of the value of the vowels in the right-hand side:
B 2; R 18; T 20; H 8; L 12;
M 13; W 23 … Total 96
A 1; O 15; O 15; E 5 … Total 36

3 (SCORE 1 POINT IF BOTH ARE CORRECT; ½ POINT IF 1 IS CORRECT.)
(A) 5; (B) 1
There are 20 teeth on A and 30 on B.
     The large annular ring will rotate in the same direction as the driving pinion.
     (A) After 4 revolutions of A the outer ring will rotate counter-clockwise through 80 teeth, causing the idling pinion to rotate through 2 revolutions (60 teeth) and an additional 20 teeth.
     (B) The driving pinion will rotate through 30 teeth —the same number as on the idling pinion, which will bring the black tooth on B to where it was originally (1).

4 20 (SCORE 1 POINT).
Even numbers have prime numbers beneath them. Prime numbers have even numbers beneath them. 17 is a prime number, and must have an even number beneath it.
     The only even number in the third line is 20.

5 A (SCORE 1 POINT).
There are three separate series. Starting with the first letter and taking every third letter thereafter:
I T A L Y
Starting with the second letter and taking every third letter thereafter:
S P A I N
From the third letter:
I N D I A

6 (SCORE 1 POINT IF ALL ARE CORRECT; ½ POINT IF 6 OR 7 ARE CORRECT.)
food
CHAIN
letter
HEAD
strong
BOX
string
BEAN
bag
PIPE
bomb
SHELL
shock
WAVE
length
WISE
crack

7 B (SCORE 1 POINT).
Removing blocks x and y leaves the following:

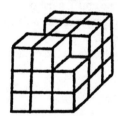

Turned upside-down, this corresponds with B.

8 D (SCORE 1 POINT).
When adjusted, the clocks show the following times:
A   from   3:27 to 12:57
B   from 11:13 to 12:13
C   from   1:44 to 12:24
D   from 10:32 to 11:52
E   from   5:21 to 12:19

9 2 4 12 (SCORE 1 POINT IF ALL ARE CORRECT; ½ POINT IF 2 ARE CORRECT.)

The first number equals the number of CENTER spots.

The second number is the total of the spots that surround the center spots.

The third number is the total of the remaining spots.

10 0 (SCORE 1 POINT).

There are three separate series, though digits representing tens are not placed adjacent to the units. For example, 12 is shown as 1 2. Starting with the first term, each third term thereafter multiplies the previous term by 3:

2 - - 6 - - - - 18 - - - - -

Starting with the second term, each third term thereafter multiplies the previous term by 4:

- 3 - - 12 - - - - 48 - - -

Starting with the third term, each third term thereafter multiplies the previous term by 5:

- - 4 - - - 20 - - - - 100.

The final term (to complete 100) is 0.

11 SUBMARINES HAVE BEEN SIGHTED IN THE NORTH ATLANTIC (SCORE 1 POINT).

From the sum on the right it is obvious that S is 7. It must be decided whether the middle one is an addition or a subtraction, but it cannot be an addition, because it would then have a three-digit answer. As it must be a subtraction, E must be 6 and T must be 1.

The left-hand problem must be an addition, so B must be 5 and A must be 9.

Substituting these letters in the code:

S - B - A - - - E S
- A - E
B E E -
S - - - T E -
- - T - E
- - - T -
A T - A - T - -

Certain words now become apparent, such as SUBMARINES and ATLANTIC.

The third word (4 letters) and the sixth word (3 letters) are worth considering:

B E E - T - E

The first must be BEEr or BEEN, and the second must be THE, TIE, or TOE. As it is unlikely that the seventh word ends in TI or TO, but could probably end in TH, it is reasonable to assume that the sixth word is THE. By substituting H wherever it occurs:

S - B - A - - N E S H A - E B E E N S _ _ H T E - - N T H E
N - - T H A T - A N T _ _

Even if by now the other words do not become apparent, the last word should be obvious:

A T - A N T - -

(remembering that it is a naval code).

This will supply L, I, and C, and the rest should fall into place.

12 (C) (SCORE 1 POINT).

SIGHING contains three letters in alphabetical order—GHI.

All the others contain three letters in reverse alphabetical order:

(A) oUTStrip
(B) rED-Currant
(D) selF-EDucated
(E) biG FEet
(F) irONMan

13 (D) (SCORE 1 POINT).

(A) would show $200 interest;
(B) would show $182 interest;
(C) would show $189 interest;
(D) would show $210 interest.

14 A is 8; B is 7; C is 11 (SCORE 1 POINT IF ALL ARE CORRECT).

Starting at the octagon (11) at the top left and moving clockwise, add the number of sides to the figure to the number of sides on its adjacent figure.

The figure before A is a pentagon (5 sides) and has a value of 9 (5 added to A, which is a square). Therefore, A (4 sides) is added to B (also 4 sides), giving A a value of 8.

B (4 sides) is added to C (a triangle), giving B a value of 7.

C (3 sides) is added to the next figure (an octagon), giving C a value of 11.

15 (SCORE 1 POINT IF ALL ARE CORRECT; ½ POINT IF 7 OR 8 ARE CORRECT.)

1 XENOPHOBE
2 EXPURGATE
3 TAXIDERMY
4 UNEXPIRED
5 UNTAXABLE
6 HYDROXIDE
7 PILLBOXES
8 ORTHODOXY
9 LETTERBOX

Remember to record your score.

NOTES

Question number 5 was another example of a "multiple" series, in which every third factor was taken, instead of every consecutive one. Your previous experience of this type of series may have helped you out.

A great deal of time had to be spent on numbers 8, 11, and 13. 13, of course, could have been solved much faster with the aid of a calculator. Incidentally, the amounts given in the answer ignore decimal fractions.

Hardly anybody succeeded with number 9—not surprising, since there was little beyond sheer inspiration to guide you on your way.

In case I am accused—in number 11— of not giving a totally unambiguous solution to every coded letter, I can only claim that, since it was a naval code, S - B - A - - N - E S and A T - A N T - - could reasonable be assumed to lead to SUBMARINES and ATLANTIC. The seventh word, (NORTH), with only - - - T H to go on, could not have been south, as S had already been accounted for. Finally, H A - E (following a plural word) could be taken as HAVE.

1 What goes into the brackets?

31 (68216) 48
19 (28184) 42
36 ( ) 47

2 Can you make anything of this?

3 What goes into the vacant square?

me	ke	ep	ua	bb	cr	at	an
de	sq	ri	mo	sa	di	le	

4 Which piece completes the jigsaw puzzle?

5 What comes next?

1⅔ 2•75 3•8 4⅚ 5⁶⁄₇ 6•875 -

6 What letter should fill the empty space?

7 In four years I shall be five times as old as I was sixteen years ago. How old am I?

8 Which letter is in the wrong line?

AHIMOSTUVWXY
BCDEFGJKLNPQRZ

9 All these vanes move 90 degrees at a time. The longer ones rotate clockwise, first one move, then missing one and moving two (that is, through 180 degrees), then missing two and moving three, and so on.

At the same time the shorter ones rotate counter-clockwise in the same way.

What will be their positions after six moves?

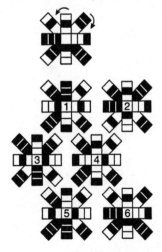

10 The black ball moves one position at a time clockwise.

If it stops on an even number, the white ball moves one position clockwise.

If it stops on an odd number, the white ball moves two positions counter-clockwise.

On what number will both balls be in the same position?

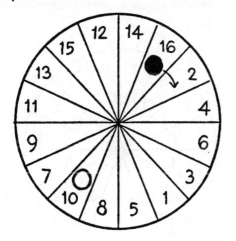

11 What comes next?

13   122   83   314   305   3   163

12 A color is concealed in each of these sentences:

(A) Temper or anger are signs of weakness.
(B) The money is for Edward.
(C) You'll find I got it elsewhere.
(D) One dancer, I see, is out of step.
(E) "I'm a gent and a lady's man," he said.

13 Find a word that fits the first definition and then, by changing one letter only, a word that fits the second definition.

(A) RADIO	INDEFATIGABLE
(B) TRAIN	REMAINDER
(C) PERSON HELD FOR RANSOM	PAYMENT FOR MAIL
(D) PENITENT	DEVISE
(E) RECOIL	MOTION OF WAVE
(F) KNEAD	COMMUNICATION
(G) WEDLOCK	DEPORTMENT
(H) MODIFY STATEMENT	DEGREE OF EXCELLENCE
(I) NAVAL VESSEL	IDOLIZE
(J) YIELD	MOST DIFFICULT

14 Here are six clocks turned upside-down. Without turning the page right side-up, which shows the nearest time to 2:25 if held in front of a mirror?

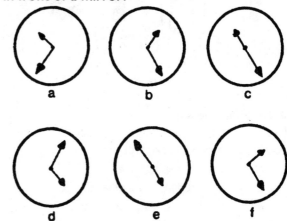

15 Complete the last line:

17	(35)	19
22	(46)	26
31	(65)	37
44	(92)	52
-	(-)	-

NOW CHECK YOUR ANSWERS AND RECORD YOUR SCORE.

1 681214 (SCORE 1 POINT).

The left-hand digit of the number on the left of the brackets is doubled to give the first digit inside the brackets.

The left-hand digit of the number on the right of the brackets is doubled to give the second digit inside the brackets.

The right-hand digit of the number on the left of the brackets is doubled to give the second number inside the brackets.

The right-hand digit of the number on the right of the brackets is doubled to give the next number inside the brackets.

2 THIS (SCORE 1 POINT).

Move the top pieces to the left and down. Move the bottom pieces to the right and up.

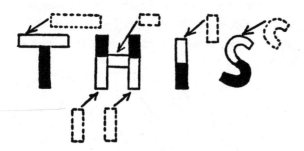

3 ke (SCORE 1 POINT).

From the top left quarter in the first square, move one position counter-clockwise throughout:

| me | ri | di | an |

Use the same procedure in the other quarters:

de	mo	cr	at
sq	ua	bb	le
ke	ep	sa	ke

4 B (SCORE 1 POINT).

5 (SCORE 1 POINT.)

Express all the terms as uneven fractions:

1⅔ 2¾ 3⅕ 4⅚ 5⁶⁄₇ 6⅞

Now it is obvious that the terms progress like this:

123 234 345 456 567 678 -

and that the final term must be 789, expressed as an uneven fraction as in the examples:

7 8/9

6 L (SCORE 1 POINT).

Starting from C, read the opposite letter (A) and then return to the opposite side, moving clockwise to the next position (T). This gives CAT.

Following this procedure:

DOG   PIG   SOW   BUL(L)

Below is shown the order in which the segments are considered:

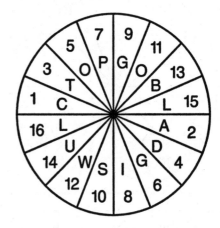

7 21 (SCORE 1 POINT).

If x represents my present age, then x + 4 = 5(x − 16). Therefore:

x + 4 = 5x − 80, from which: 84 = 4x, so x = 21.

8 S (SCORE 1 POINT).

All the letters in the top line except S will read the same if reflected in a mirror.

S should be in the bottom line, in which every letter would read backwards if reflected in a mirror.

9 5 (SCORE 1 POINT).

10 15 (SCORE 1 POINT).

The balls move as follows:

Black ball	White ball
2	7
4	9
6	11
3	7
1	8
5	1
8	5
10	8
7	1
9	6
11	2
13	14
15	15

11 0 (SCORE 1 POINT).

Correctly spaced, the series becomes:

1 31 2 28 3 31 4 30 5 31 6 3 -

The series is based on the days and months of the year—the month followed by the number of days. June has 30 days, so the final term should be 30.

12 (SCORE 1 POINT IF ALL ARE CORRECT).

(A) ORANGE
(B) RED
(C) INDIGO
(D) CERISE
(E) MAGENTA

13 (SCORE 1 POINT IF ALL ARE CORRECT; ½ POINT IF 8 OR 9 ARE CORRECT.)

(A) WIRELESS	TIRELESS
(B) RETINUE	RESIDUE
(C) HOSTAGE	POSTAGE
(D) CONTRITE	CONTRIVE
(E) BACKLASH	BACKWASH
(F) MASSAGE	MESSAGE
(G) MARRIAGE	CARRIAGE
(H) QUALIFY	QUALITY
(I) WARSHIP	WORSHIP
(J) HARVEST	HARDEST

14 d (SCORE 1 POINT).

15 (SCORE 1 POINT.)

The numbers on each side of the brackets alternately increase by 2, 3, 4, 5, 6, 7, 8 (and then 9 and 10). To discover the number inside the brackets: double the number on the left and add 1, then 2, then 3, then 4, and finally 5 (122 plus 5 - 127).

Remember to record your score.

NOW TOTAL ALL YOUR SCORES FOR THE THREE TESTS IN THIS SECTION AND CHECK YOUR IQ ON THE IQ CHART IN THE BACK OF THE BOOK.

NOTES

The volunteers experienced greatest difficulty with 3, 6, 9, and 11, though, in the case of 11, they were warned to look out for series which are incorrectly spaced. When the series is spaced correctly, the relationship between the months and days becomes apparent.

The important clue to solving number 3 was the fact that q is always followed by u. This leads to the fact that SQ in square 1 must be followed by UA in the next square. This combination may have pointed to the order in which all the letters were positioned.

In the Answers, I offer an algebraic solution to number 7, though it can be solved by trial and error. Unless you are lucky, algebra offers the quickest solution.

The most time-consuming problems were 3, 9, 13, and (in particular) 10.

RATINGS IN GROUP III

Test 1   Average 4$\frac{1}{2}$ points

Test 2   Average 5 points

Test 3   Average 5$\frac{1}{2}$ points

TOTAL FOR THE GROUP

Out of a possible 45 points:

Over 30   Excellent

22–29   Very good

16–21   Good

15   Average

10–14   Fair

Under 10   Poor

Although the average score was very low, it must be acknowledged that many of the problems in this group were very difficult. However, a few problems which completely baffled the majority of test-takers were solved with relative ease by some—once again proving the point that aptitude has a major influence on the results. Those who fared well in the numerical tests may have done badly on the verbal tests, and so on.

Now find your overall total score for all the tests, and find your IQ on the IQ chart at the back of the book.

IQ SCORING INSTRUCTIONS

Count up the number of correct answers you came up with on the tests in each of the test levels you attempted. Find your approximate IQ score in the extreme right hand column. You may measure your IQ after taking one category of tests, or look at the sum of your scores for all of the test levels for a more accurate, composite score.

NOTE: This chart is based on test-takers who are 16 years or older. If you are younger than 16, add 10 points to your score for each year your age falls below 16.

YOUR ELEMENTARY TEST SCORE	YOUR CHALLENGING TEST SCORE	YOUR MASTERFUL TEST SCORE	YOUR COMPOSITE TEST SCORE	YOUR APPROXIMATE IQ SCORE
60	60	45	165	140
59½	59	44½	163	138
59	57	44	160	136
58½	56	43½	158	134
57½	55	43	155	132
56½	54	42	152	130
56	53	41	150	128
55	52	40½	147	126
54½	51	40	145	124
54	49½	39	142	122
53	48	38	139	120
52	46	36½	134	118
50½	44	35	129	116
49	42	33½	124	114
47	40	31½	118	112
45½	38	30	113	110
44	36	28½	108	108
42½	34	27	103	106
41	32	25½	98	104
39½	30	24	93	102
37½	28½	23	89	100
36	27½	22	85	98
34½	26½	21	82	96
33	25½	20	78	94
31½	24½	19	75	92
30	23½	18	71	90
28½	22½	17	68	88
27	21½	16	64	86
25½	20½	15	61	84
24	19½	14	57½	82
22½	18½	13	54	80
21	17½	12	50	78
19½	16½	11	47	76
18	15½	10	43	74
16½	14½	9	40	72
15	13	8	36	70